Caring communities

A challenge for social inclusion

Alan Barr, Carolyn Stenhouse and Paul Henderson

The **Joseph Rowntree Foundation** has supported this project as part of its programme of research and innovative development projects, which it hopes will be of value to policy makers and practitioners. The facts presented and views expressed in this report are, however, those of the authors and not necessarily those of the Foundation.

Findings of an action-research project funded by the Joseph Rowntree Foundation and the Scottish Executive Social Work Services Inspectorate

Published for the Joseph Rowntree Foundation by YPS

ISBN 1 84263 017 2

Prepared and printed by:
York Publishing Services Ltd
64 Hallfield Road
Layerthorpe
York
YO31 7ZQ
Tel: 01904 430033   Fax: 01904 430868   E-mail: orders@yps.ymn.co.uk

Contents

Acknowledgements

The research team could not have captured the richness and detail of community and user involvement without having had the enthusiastic support of a wide range of individuals and organisations in each of the four project sites. We are grateful for the commitment shown by volunteers, members of community and voluntary organisations, and by the staff – practitioners and managers – employed in the areas by the four local authorities and key voluntary agencies involved. The project asked a great deal: requests for information and interviews, completing questionnaires, extra meetings in the localities as well as a 24-hour cross-site workshop, reading drafts, talking through issues. All of this and more was given with great generosity.

Equally important has been the willingness of the four local authorities with which we worked to sustain their commitment during the lifetime of the project: staff members from across each of the authorities, representing a variety of departments and positions, have helped us, and we are grateful both to them and to those in the authorities who took the decision originally to collaborate with the project.

We are also grateful to the Joseph Rowntree Foundation and the Scottish Executive Social Work Services Inspectorate both for funding the project and for giving it their active support. Alex O'Neil from the Foundation chaired the project's Advisory Group, and we would like to thank him for his willingness to accommodate changes in the project as it developed as well as the personal and intellectual support he gave. Similarly, other members of the Advisory Group (listed in Appendix 3) gave unstinting attention to the project and helped guide the project's direction. We particularly wish to thank Neil Small who, towards the end of the project, took on an additional consultancy role for the project.

Finally, Karen McKelvie and Frances Stewart at the Scottish Community Development Centre provided an essential administrative base for the project. We appreciate the way in which they did this as well as the support they gave.

Executive summary

1   *Caring Communities: a Challenge for Social Inclusion* reports on a three-year action-research project on the contribution of a community development approach to community care.

2   The project was funded by the Joseph Rowntree Foundation and the Social Work Services Inspectorate of the Scottish Executive and was undertaken, in partnership with four local authorities in Scotland, by a research team based at the Scottish Community Development Centre. The four sites or areas studied were: Kincardine, a village in Fife; minority ethnic communities in part of Glasgow; a disability strategy group in South Lanarkshire; and the work of a voluntary organisation in Lochaber, Highland.

3   The dominant theme underlying the project's more detailed findings is the connection between community-based initiatives in the field of community care with other issues which are of concern to local people. This conclusion from the experiences of four communities relates directly to the Government's commitment to tackling social exclusion, notably by insisting that local authorities work in partnership with communities. It is urging them and other agencies to adopt 'joined-up' solutions to 'joined-up' problems. There was evidence from the action-research that this policy thrust is impacting already on the way in which agencies and communities work together.

4   Crucial to using a community development approach effectively in the context of caring communities is the need for all stakeholders to play an active role: community leaders, service users, frontline workers and managers each have distinctive contributions to make, but they are also interdependent: if one or more groups is weak or marginalised then the whole approach will be jeopardised.

5   Community leaders and practitioners in the four areas gave clear indications of the key factors that are required for effective practice by local authorities and others:
  • build on what exists already
  • ensure that serious attention is given to assessing community needs especially as they are experienced by local people
  • actively involve senior and middle managers in planning and operationalising the approach
  • make use of knowledge available on the ingredients for successful partnerships
  • locate the care needs of communities within a corporate, social inclusion framework rather than only within the community care legislation, making use of community development principles, values and methods.

6   The project reaffirmed the extent of commitment to be found among communities to work together on shared issues, and the contribution that community development can make to supporting caring communities within a clear social inclusion framework. The ultimate goal is the creation of stronger communities.

7   The research team recommends that the thinking of local authorities and other agencies which are responsible for planning community care should in future be informed by the overall conclusion of the action-research, namely that the development of caring communities presents a major challenge for social inclusion. Three specific recommendations put forward are:
  • the preparation and dissemination of guidelines for good practice
  • provision of training opportunities for senior managers, frontline workers, community leaders and users on key elements required for the implementation of a community-based approach

- a national policy seminar and local policy conferences designed to clarify how to take forward the challenge of caring communities within a social inclusion framework.

1 Context and purpose

A new social policy language has permeated the planning and policymaking of local authorities and other agencies across the UK. In place of 'poverty' and 'deprivation' the terms 'social exclusion'/ 'social inclusion' and community-based regeneration are driving the policy agenda, led in England by the Social Exclusion Unit's National Strategy for Neighbourhood Renewal and being replicated in the other three nations.

The findings of the action-research project contained in this report fit within the new policy framework:

- The project began with a focus on the application of community development approaches to community care.

- During its three years, the project observed and recorded a shift of focus in the four sites studied from an exploration of the contribution of community development to community care to a more holistic approach whereby community care is located within a broader framework of community concerns.

- The action-research was able to record the impact of the new social policy agenda on both local agencies and communities.

There was, therefore, a dynamic relationship between the experiences and aspirations of the four communities supported and observed by the research team and government policy statements.

Running alongside the social policy imperatives of social inclusion and regeneration is growing evidence from across the country of some of the potential and problems associated with encouraging community involvement. Issues around setting up and sustaining community participation in local partnerships is one example of a problem area. The findings of the action-research are as important here as they are for the policy debate: on the one hand, the experiences of local communities, how they organise themselves and how they engage with a range of statutory and voluntary organisations; on the other, the presence and skills of practitioners who support local communities.

It is the themes of social inclusion and community involvement which provide the overall context for the action-research findings. In terms of the more focused context, it is the development of community care policies and how they are delivered in and with communities that concerned the action-research. The study was a critically important phase in a process of researching and debating ways in which community care can become more than just the provision of services to individuals within severe budgetary constraints. It was critical because, having clarified the arguments for a community development approach to community care, and having undertaken a mapping of conceptual and operational issues (see Appendix 1), it was necessary to find out whether or not such an approach could work. Thus the purpose of the action-research was to:

1   develop a planned demonstration project in partnership with four local authorities

2   provide training, consultancy and evaluation support to the four projects, using a participative style

3   identify whether or not the benefits of a community development approach to community care can be demonstrated by focusing on:
    - personal change in participants (users and providers)
    - change in the ability of user communities to influence or control services
    - changes in policy and practice of service agencies with particular regard to accountability and user participation
    - changes in the level of consumer satisfaction
    - changes in the efficiency and effectiveness of the use of resources

- changes in levels and quality of collaboration between users, communities and service agencies.

The research team members held the view that it was important to distinguish between user involvement and community development, arguing, on the basis of their earlier research, that the activities are overlapping and congruent. The action-research gave particular attention to the extension of user involvement into full citizen participation.

Historically, community development has had close connections with social work. Over the last 20 years, however, the link between the two has been relatively weak: community development has been drawn into the economic development and regeneration fields (Taylor, 1995). The social work profession, on the other hand, has had to respond to new legislation (including that for community care) and pressures. In this sense, the focus of the action-research was reconnecting community development to themes and issues, located primarily within a social work framework, which had received only minimal attention. However, as indicated above, the findings of the action-research have taken the project out of a social work context into a broader social inclusion framework. It is within this framework that, by and large, community development work in the UK is now operating (Henderson and Salmon, 2000). Will it be through this route that community development will rediscover its links with social work?

Key themes

Based on the empirical evidence of the projects, the report highlights a need to establish effective community care as a key dimension of policy and practice for social inclusion. The extent to which this requires a shift in assumptions about care in the community should not be underestimated.

Policy analysts might be surprised if they were asked to envisage a close connection between the concepts of community care and social inclusion. They have very different points of origin.

The policy of care in the community has been part of British social policy for over 50 years. It moved up the political and policy agendas from the end of the 1980s as, arguably, a pragmatic response to the increasing costs and pressures of institutional care allied with a general feeling that vulnerable people needed to be offered choices other than long-stay hospitals and residential institutions.

The term social exclusion originated in French social policy and is widely used by the European Union as well as in the UK. It is distinct from the term poverty because it encompasses the idea of inequality and because it draws attention to peoples' experiences of being outside mainstream society – the excluded, the marginalised. Social exclusion is more than a material condition. It is a multidimensional concept, 'embracing a variety of ways in which people may be denied full participation in society and full effective rights of citizenship in the civil, political and social spheres' (Lister, 1999). The term social inclusion gets closer to the idea of active participation than the term social exclusion: action taken by people to improve living conditions and to bring about change.

The connection between community care and social exclusion emerges from different influences. In all the sites, there were local policies relating to the Government's social inclusion and 'modernising government' agendas. These emphasise the need for interdisciplinary and cross-sectoral collaboration, community participation and citizen involvement and, in some cases, decentralisation of services and decision making. 'Joined-up', responsive and participative governance is an important theme into which, arguably, the community care agenda is being drawn. The implications for practice have provoked debate about the core ideas which should be informing governance, including community care.

The experience of the projects was that, from a community and service user perspective, issues relating specifically to community care services could not be conveniently isolated from many others that determined the quality of personal or community life. Exclusion was a powerful common denominator between care users and others in the community. Needs were consistently placed in a context that connected them to wider community concerns related, for example, to transport, safety, planning, leisure opportunities, accessible services or responsive governance. A capacity to participate effectively in and influence policy and services depended on recognition of exclusion from full citizenship and the need for collective organisation and partnerships rather than the dominant characteristics of community care practice – individual need assessment and efficient management of resources.

It has become increasingly apparent that the policy commitments driving the inclusion agenda are frequently in tension with a parallel emphasis on 'new managerialism' – the emphasis placed on target setting, measurable outputs and outcomes, audit trails, best value and value for money. While clarity of purpose and careful measurement of progress are highly desirable, this must not be to the exclusion of citizens from involvement in the definition of purpose, priorities and criteria for measurement.

Project sites

For reasons of accessibility and support, all the four areas on which the findings are based are in Scotland:

- Fife Council – participative approaches to community care in a large village within a council policy of decentralisation and citizen involvement

- Glasgow City Council – participation of ethnic minority carers in inner-city neighbourhoods

Map 1 The project sites

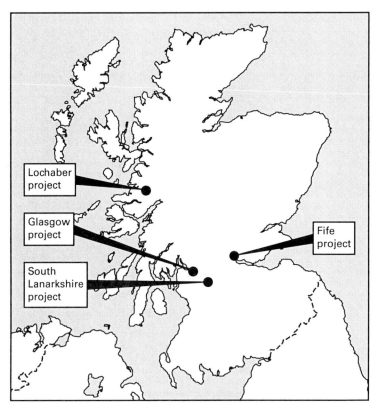

- South Lanarkshire Council – council-wide disability strategy group in partnership with community organisations

- Voluntary Action Lochaber with Highland Council and Highland Health Board – community link volunteers and care needs in remote rural communities

Funding for the project was provided by the Joseph Rowntree Foundation and the Scottish Executive Social Work Services Inspectorate. While the context and detail of the report inevitably have a clear Scottish imprint, the project was seen by the funders and the action-research team as being relevant to the whole of the UK and, as indicated above, there is no doubt that both the policy and the practice findings have this broader relevance.

Table 1 Summary of project characteristics

Variable	Fife	Glasgow	South Lanarkshire	Lochaber
Location	Large village	Inner-city neighbourhood	Extensive: rural and urban	Extensive: remote rural
User group	Generic	Carers for disabled children	Disability	Generic
Main community participants	Community leaders of local organisations	Asian carers group	Coalition of disability organisation leaders	Community-based volunteers
Main agency participants	Social work (lead agency), locality management, community services, housing, local voluntary agencies	Social work managed steering group. Limited voluntary sector involvement	Cross-department council involvement: social work, leisure, chief executives, housing, planning, education	Voluntary Action Lochaber (lead agency), social work, health board, health trust, local voluntary organisations
Focus	Promotion of a caring community through citizen participation and worker collaboration	Empowerment and service improvement for excluded carers	Achieving full citizenship for disabled people	Reaching, supporting and promoting the voice of care users in remote communities

The sites were selected following consultation with local agencies and community interests (information on the background to the action-research can be found in Appendix 1, and a summary of the research methods and the data sources used is contained in Appendix 2).

Structure

The report sets out to provide:

- an account of the work which developed in each of the project sites

- a summary of the key issues and lessons for policy makers, practitioners and community leaders.

The chapter on themes and issues stands on its own, i.e. it can be studied without first having read the case studies. However, the points made in Chapter 3 will be more meaningful if the reader is aware of the key features and main developments of the local experiences.

Each project is set in its local context and the main inputs, processes of action and consequent outputs and outcomes are described. There has been substantial work and significant progress on all four sites, but also problems to resolve. The factors that have promoted success, enabled or undermined effective problem solving reflect the constraints, opportunities and roles played by the key stakeholder groups in each project:

- community leaders (including service user leaders and volunteers)

- service users

- frontline agency staff

- agency managers.

In Chapter 3, the perspective of each group is adopted in order to focus attention on the issues that are of particular significance to them. Chapter 4 is concerned with the question of what needs to be done to put into practice the findings of the action-research. In the concluding chapter, general and specific recommendations for the development of policy and practice are proposed.

2 Caring communities: case studies

In this section, each of the projects is described with commentary from the perspectives of the key participants.

Kincardine, Fife

Kincardine is a large village (population just over 3,000) on the western edge of Fife, located at a significant bridging point on the Forth estuary and in the former Fife coalfield. Its historical association with mining, the power industry and its proximity to the oil and chemical industry across the river in Grangemouth give it more urban-industrial than rural-agricultural characteristics. It is a mixed community with an old village centre, newer private and public sector housing developments, the latter including three tower blocks of flats. Its location at a major bridging point results in heavy traffic passing though the village. Ironically, it has generally poor public transport communication to the major population and service centres in its area. This is partly because these centres, notably Falkirk, Alloa and Stirling, are in different local authority areas.

The peripheral location of Kincardine within Fife creates complications because some key services are not located in the local authority area, while others, notably the Health Board, straddle local authority boundaries. Residents have a strong sense of being on the periphery. As a result, it is felt that Kincardine does not get the attention that it should from public bodies. It was a shared perception among council officers that this might be the case that led to the village being selected as the site for the project. As one agency manager put it: 'The geographical location of the village and the Kincardine Bridge make it a place that both belongs to and is apart from the rest of Fife.'

Local authority's policies

The action-research team had prior knowledge of the policy commitment of the Labour-controlled Fife Council, on the one hand to community participation across the range of its services and, on the other, to decentralised cross-disciplinary approaches to locality management. These policies had arisen from a 'citizenship commission' established at the time of local government reorganisation in 1996. It was the commitment to 'build an authority which actively involves people in the decision making process and enables the public to shape the design of services and the way in which the council serves its communities' that attracted the action-research team.

Each service, including Social Work with its responsibility for community care, was required to: 'identify the key groups appropriate to their service which should be included within specific participative arrangements'. There was, then, a prior commitment to the kind of approach that the project was seeking to test. Consultation with senior officers in the Social Work and Chief Executives' departments led to a commitment to participate in the action-research with a project in the West Fife area. However, the final decision about location was left to discussion with local staff on a cross-departmental basis – including representatives of Social Work, Chief Executives, Community Education, Schools and Housing services. Kincardine was seen, historically, as poorly served and in need of attention. It had a newly established local multi-service office that could provide a focus for development but staff were clear that they did not wish to impose a project on the community – as one put it: 'We need to build a solid resource developed with the community.' It was partly for this reason that the project was relatively slow to develop – though there were other significant factors, including the following.

- Different perceptions about engaging with community care were held by different services. The Social Work Department aspired to a more participative approach and this was illustrated in the community care plan that talked of, 'ensuring the existence of appropriate arrangements and lines of communication so that all stakeholders including users and carers are consulted and involved in the joint planning and working process at local level'. But its activity related primarily to specific statutory obligations to assess needs and plan services for particular client groups. For other services, community care was a more general concept associated with a mutually supportive and caring community.

- There was lack of clarity about who would take the lead in the broader development. Other departments seemed to expect Social Work to take a lead. The senior social work manager for West Fife, who also held responsibilities across the department for community development, played a key role but he was not located in Kincardine. At that level, specific responsibility for championing the project was taken up by one social worker in particular whose workload and role, despite a strong commitment to community-based practice, made it difficult to provide the level of sustained activity required. These problems were not resolved for about a year.

- Despite the presence of a local council office, the concept of decentralised service development was in its infancy and workers were being affected by ongoing council restructuring and budget restrictions. Hence, much time in the early part of the project was spent clarifying roles and relationships between services. Despite the intention to build the project on community perceptions, most of the first year of the project was characterised by a continuing dialogue largely between service providers – to the exclusion of the community. Based on materials from the baseline questionnaire, the service providers drew up a general aim for the project which was:

To promote the participation of users of community care services in Kincardine, and their carers, in order to shape the quality and character of the services they receive.

Consultation

Direct involvement of the community began in small ways with the involvement of members of the Kincardine Old People's Welfare – an active organisation providing lunch club and recreational activities for older people – in meetings of the steering group of council officers. The first attempt to promote wider community involvement was a conventional exercise in consultation over the annual community care plan. Members of the community were invited to attend one of two local meetings to hear a presentation of the plan and comment on its contents. This placed the community in a highly reactive position. The plan was complex, and many of the participants were much more concerned about issues that it did not address, for example, the quality of public transport. This led to the recognition that more imaginative approaches were needed and that the agenda the community wished to address might be quite different in character from that of the council, with its statutory community care obligations. Aspects of interest overlapped, particularly in relation to the threatened closure of day-care services for older people in the area and lack of continuity and consistency of home care support.

Transformation of project

But much of the community agenda related to other things, notably, deficiencies in quality and consistency of service provided by the local office, better coordination of service provision, better resourcing of voluntary organisations, improved maternity and paediatric services, better public transport. For the community, community care was a much broader idea than a specific set of services. Participation could not be neatly slotted into the organisational responsibilities of particular council services but required a much more holistic approach. This realisation transformed the project. There was a community-driven transition from a specific focus on community care services to a broader one on creating a healthy, caring and inclusive community. This finding proved to be of critical importance for the action-research's conclusions on community care in the context of social inclusion.

It had taken a year, but, once this lesson had been learned, there was a substantial shift in approach. Workers increasingly emphasised an ongoing dialogue with local people, through both meetings with community organisations and using evidence from personal contacts in the community. The Social Work Department brought a community worker into Kincardine to work closely with the community social worker and other services, and located her in the local office. A visit with representatives of community organisations was arranged to a project in Langholm, in Dumfries and Galloway, to look at what was being done in a similar size community to assess and respond to a community agenda.

Based on the lessons from this visit, funding was made available to support a survey of local community needs carried out by a consultant in collaboration with local community activists. A further survey was conducted, primarily through frontline staff of council services, specifically on the issue of day care and support service needs in the community. The reports were used to inform continuing dialogue with the community through participative events. These were conducted in a highly imaginative manner.

Informal meetings

One was an event called 'Blether over yer Denner' where members of the Old People's Welfare lunch club could meet council and other agency staff very informally and raise any issues of concern to them. A second was called 'True Colours' and involved an open day in the Old People's Welfare, during which topics highlighted from the community survey and other sources were an ongoing focus for informal discussion with different people from the community over the day. Issues were recorded, ideas encouraged and proposals for action fed into continuing discussion of the project steering group.

Local staff and those with a strategic function, such as the community care planner who was an active participant, felt that genuine communication with local people on their terms and relating to their priorities was established and better informed the responses of the council.

The following comments from local people who attended these events highlight their value:

The format of the 'Blether' meetings was really good – those people who probably would never have gone to the council office or faced up to someone who was an official went along and had their say…Public meetings are intimidating for people to speak at but in the 'Blether' format we could make our point or ask a question over a cup of tea. (Sequence Dance Organiser)

The meetings really worked – they were informal and people covered everything from the days the bins are collected to 'my home help doesn't come at the time stated'. (Bowling Club Member)

The meetings improved relationships and the perception of the council. (Lunch Club Volunteer)

Positive views of these events were also held by council officers. One commented particularly on the benefits of openness with residents about financial constraints on the council. While this was not seen as a reason to restrict community demands, it was nonetheless noted that: 'If communities have information on budgets and limitations they are able to make sensible decisions without huge monetary implications.'

Community representatives were now equally involved in the project steering group. Supports to community groups were being provided through the local office, including: a directory of local organisations called 'Groupscope'; a calendar of community events; a series of meetings with a local reporter called 'Press don't bite'; and information exchange though a community notice board.

Community focus

A network group of workers, called the Community Action Team, with an involvement in supporting community care users, was established. It included council staff, WRVS (Women's Royal Voluntary Service), the local assistant pharmacist and health visitor. This group began to meet regularly to share information to enhance preventive practice. The assistant pharmacist said of it:

It has really improved relationships and contacts. I never used to see the health visitor, but now we make a point of seeing each other once or twice a week. I've learned so much about all the other services and we all share information and build local contacts ... we're all so good at picking up on cases that we're concerned about and whether it is the WRVS, the church or a social worker, someone would respond.

The local office was used as a work base and contact point for people in the community. A community newsletter and information board helped groups and individuals to contact one another. From being a council facility, the office came to be more of a community focus. As one agency worker put it:

Some local office staff have started to make the link that local groups may be able to assist in resolving issues and queries.

From a stuttering start, the project began to have a significant influence on community life. Community care in its traditional sense was incorporated into a wider approach to the needs of Kincardine as a whole.

Achievements and frustrations

At the stage of the final review of the project, community members pointed to important improvements including:

- the level of involvement of people in the village especially because of the innovative approaches taken to participation

- improved access to and level of services particularly through the local office – 'people are now clear where they can go to and what they can obtain' (Local Volunteer)

- increased trust between service providers and local organisations and volunteers –'Social Work input was outstanding – local workers input was immense' (Volunteer)

- better information about the village as a result of the surveys – 'Everyone involved knows a lot more about what Kincardine people want.' (Volunteer)

- better contact with isolated people

- transport service now being on the council agenda – 'the new community bus has helped folk get out in the evening, clubs are now really well attended' (Member of the Darby and Joan Club)

- improvements in the delivery of home-care services through the development of home-care teams.

There were also frustrations, in particular about:

- the continued threat of closure of the local day-care facility

- continuing transport difficulties

- the need for traffic management and a new bridge

- the need for better coordination between health and social work services and more involvement from health services.

Views of successes were largely shared by the agency staff. Frontline workers felt particularly positive about the changed working relationships that had developed not only between council staff but also with others including voluntary organisations such as the WRVS, the health visitor and the pharmacist. They talked of 'developed trust' and 'sense of teamwork in the community'. Managers emphasised improved communication with the community, better informed services, improved identity for Kincardine within the council and welcomed their direct engagement in the community through participatory events. Improving the relevance and satisfaction with services was believed to be a cost-effective way of working.

Both groups of staff would have liked more extensive and broader-based community involvement, including greater participation in service provision, better participation from health services and some council services. Frontline workers wanted more recognition from managers of the demands of the approach, and some managers were critical of their own role. In response to the lack of Health Board participation, one senior council manager said: 'Apart from the health visitor there was no involvement whatever – they had decided long ago that none of this was relevant.' In relation to the participation of operational and strategic managers, another said: 'Only a small number of senior managers have demonstrated a consistent commitment.'

The project is ongoing. There are difficulties to resolve but, from slow beginnings, major changes in approach have been adopted with corresponding outcomes in relation to the community. As much as anything, these arise from a change in style and perhaps even in working culture in the locality. As an agency community worker put it: 'This work has reminded me of the importance of a simple focus for community work and a non-prescriptive approach ... to enable all potential stakeholders to get involved on their terms *not* the council's, Government, whoever!'

Glasgow

The City of Glasgow is the largest in Scotland and, though its population was cut by local government reorganisation in 1996 to approximately 600,000, it is the hub of a conurbation of well over two million people. As a major industrial and commercial centre, its history has seen successive migrations both internally within Scotland, from elsewhere in the UK and Ireland and, more recently, from other parts of the world (though often via other parts of the UK). Glasgow has the largest black and ethnic minority population of any Scottish city, accounting for approximately 3.5 per cent of the population (21,000 people). Half of this group were born in Scotland, and the proportion rises all the time.

As in other cities, there are significant socio-economic differences within the minority ethnic communities, though generally they experience relative poverty and are primarily located in more disadvantaged inner-city neighbourhoods. The predominant place of family origin is Pakistan, with a sizeable Indian population, a smaller but significant Chinese community, but a relatively small Afro-Caribbean group. In Glasgow, it was the care needs of minority ethnic communities that became the focus of the project.

Community workers

In Glasgow, the Social Work Department had a long-standing commitment to community development approaches, inherited from its predecessor authority, Strathclyde Regional Council. As a result of the severe financial pressures that Glasgow has experienced, the number of community workers has been reduced by half since local government reorganisation. Yet, community workers remain a significant part of the workforce. Their remit, however, has moved from a generic one, in which their task was to assist communities to organise around any local concern, to one focused on supporting initiatives relating to the mainstream responsibilities of social work, particularly in relation to community care and children and families.

Although there had been a long-standing policy commitment to community development approaches to community care, relatively little sustained practice had occurred.

The action-research project coincided with the change in focus adopted in Glasgow and was seen as an opportunity to test out community development approaches in community care. The Social Work Department suggested two options.[1] Partly because there was known to be a low uptake of services, but also because it broadened the scope of the action-research, a focus on ethnic minorities was selected. Within this, a particular interest was expressed in mental health issues though, as the project developed, this became less central. The department set as its broad aim:

To support users of services and carers from black and ethnic minority communities to participate in planning, development and delivery of services which will meet their needs in an accessible and appropriate way.

From the start, the initiative was located primarily in the Social Work Department and promoted through a steering group chaired by a senior manager. Initially, it had been proposed that the work would focus in the area of just one social work team, but it rapidly became evident that the administrative boundaries were of little relevance to community identities of ethnic minorities located across the inner-city and falling within the locus of at least three teams. The steering group therefore rapidly developed to encompass the area team managers and community work staff from each of the teams.

Each team manager identified an initiative resulting, in effect, in three sub-projects. One was already under way and was focusing on developmental support to Asian carers of children with disabilities in two adjacent neighbourhoods. A second would build on established work with a community-run day-care centre for

Chinese elders, and focus on dementia. The third would explore issues of stress relating to young people in the Sikh community and build on established links with a local Gudwara (Sikh temple). In practice, only the first of these developed into a substantial and sustained project. It is important, however, to comment briefly on the others.

Sikh young people

In the case of the Sikh young people, discussion at the Gudwara with young people had highlighted a concern about aspects of racism and cultural identity that represented stressful life experiences and events. How to combat these was a matter in which young people expressed interest. The discussion led to a workshop run in partnership with a community arts project and, subsequently, an eight-session group work programme in which the young people used drama, improvisation, role play and video to explore experiences of racism and stress. However, under tight resource restrictions, the initiative was not sustained or linked to any wider programme.

Chinese day-care centre

The work with the Wing Hong Chinese elderly day-care centre was more substantial. The centre has been operational for ten years and is a very positive illustration of community development support to direct community provision of services. It has an elected executive committee drawn from the Chinese community, membership of over 500 and regular participation of 160 Chinese elders. It employs directly or in partnership with the council 12 staff, both full time and sessional. It describes itself as promoting 'equal opportunity for elderly Chinese in access to various social, health, welfare and housing services' and 'a complementary channel to mainstream services and care provisions so that their specific needs can be met'. Throughout its operation, it has had close involvement with the Social Work Department, which is a key funder.

Following a report by the Royal College of Nursing and Thames Valley University (Foong and Walsh, 1995), centre staff had highlighted concern about the inadequacy of service responses to mental health issues for their users. The report drew attention to a lack of awareness of available services and the problems of communication with service providers. But it was pointed out that the services were often unresponsive or seen as inappropriate by the Chinese community because of differences in conception of mental health in Chinese and Western thought and lack of familiarity with, or confidence in, approaches such as counselling or psychotherapy.

Problems of a user-led approach

As a result of a concern about the probability of an inadequate response to need, the Social Work Department had worked with the centre to audit the mental health needs of the members and identified a hidden problem relating to functional mental illness and dementia. Finding an appropriate response was less easy, but it was felt that, especially given the different view taken of mental illness within the community, a user-led approach would be appropriate.

However, though the centre was managed by members of the Chinese community, its practice was not characterised by direct involvement of its users. To take a user empowerment approach, and to do so in the context of the complexities of the issue of mental health within the Chinese community, was therefore simultaneously to address two demanding areas for change. Add to this a lack of available Chinese-speaking staff with community development and community care expertise and progress was always likely to be difficult. Attempts to establish a mental health user group foundered, and a review of progress suggested that the desire to create a participative, user-led approach might actually be increasing rather than tackling the stresses of users.

In the light of this, it was decided to withdraw from this approach. The centre, in collaboration with Social Work, the Health Board and the local association for mental health would focus on how a more effective response could be made to individual needs. A middle manager in the Social Work Department commented:

It was evident through the efforts to develop work with the Wing Hong how the work was inhibited by the lack of a bilingual worker with community work skills and the lack of an ongoing relationship between community work and that community.

It is important not simply to dismiss this initiative as a failure. Certainly, the collective user empowerment approach was not successful, but the attempt to adopt it highlighted and enhanced understanding of a range of issues from which it became apparent that other methods of intervention were, at the time and in the specific circumstances, more appropriate. It is always important to review critically the relevance of different methods of intervention and to be aware of the resources and conditions that will enable them to be successful. The decision to withdraw from the community development approach was based on reflective assessment. However, the inappropriateness of the approach in some contexts does not negate its validity in others, as was clearly demonstrated by the work in Glasgow with ethnic minority carers.

Asian carers project

The work with ethnic minority carers was developed in two adjacent inner-city neighbourhoods, Govanhill and Pollokshields. It was described by a participant as: 'to encourage carers to organise structures that would allow them to promote their own interests'.

The predominant minority ethnic group is Muslim and of Pakistani origin. The area is now served by a single social work team. 1991 Census figures indicate that 40 per cent of the population in Pollokshields (3,032) rising to 61 per cent (of which 48 per cent were of Pakistani origin) in East Pollokshields, and 18 per cent (1,434) in neighbouring Govanhill are from black and minority ethnic communities.

Despite a predominance of owner occupation, it is noteworthy – as an indicator of deprivation – that 75 per cent of all households in the joint area are in receipt of housing benefit. In East Pollokshields, which has been the primary focus of the work, there is a high proportion of young people (50 per cent under the age of 25), and there is evident interracial tension particularly among this group. In the Pakistani community, Punjabi is the predominant language.

The area provides a range of commercial, religious, cultural and other services specifically oriented to the minority ethnic communities. Historically, community organisations have been largely led by men, whereas the carers group was largely led by women. There have been several service initiatives in the area, including a multicultural centre, a youth counselling service, a development agency and an advocacy and home care service. The last of these is the only one closely linked to the development of the project and was run by Barnardos, which later became a significant partner in the initiative.

Earlier work

The Social Work Department area office is located outside the area, but there is a local outreach office in East Pollokshields that has historically been a location for community work and advice and information staff and was seen by all participants as of importance in the success of the project. At the time of the project, there were five community work staff for the whole area of Govanhill and

Pollokshields: three white, qualified community workers (one of whom had a managerial role) and two minority ethnic, bilingual community work assistants.

Work by community work staff with carers pre-dated the action-research project, having begun in Govanhill in 1995, before a reorganisation of social work teams that led to Govanhill and Pollokshields being a focus for the same team. The area social work team had reviewed the uptake of services by members of the minority ethnic communities and found that, with the exception of occupational therapy services, they were substantially under-represented. Around the same time, the Community Relations Council expressed concern about the need for improvement in services for children with special needs. A senior social worker (community care) worked with community workers and occupational therapists to identify carers in the community. From an initial contact group of 20, the formation of a new carer group was encouraged.

This group continued to meet for about two and a half years. The main service improvement was social work provision of a respite care scheme for children. However, by the summer of 1997, members were no longer showing the same interest and the local office in which it met was closed with the reorganisation of social work services and reduced availability of local support.

In East Pollokshields, staff had also identified a low uptake in council services by members of the minority ethnic community. In 1997, coinciding with the start of the action-research, community work staff proposed a process of dialogue with the minority ethnic communities that began with a survey of carers of children with special needs. Work with carers provided a good opportunity for contact with the new area team manager as well as social work staff in community care and children and families teams. Community workers took the lead in the project, seeking to discuss with carers their views on existing social work services, to identify carer needs and to stimulate interest in the establishment of a carers group.

This led to the development of a group with a regular attendance of around 20 and, for special meetings, nearer 40. The group had a direct influence on service provision for individual families involved as well as those in the wider community. In particular, it gained support funding, from both Social Work and voluntary agencies, for a respite care playscheme planned by the group with community worker support. It brought about change in social work practice and the nature of service delivery from both statutory and voluntary agencies operating in the area. For example, the area manager met regularly with the group, community care and childcare staff began to attend group meetings, and occupational therapy staff provided surgeries at health centres. Sensitivity to the experiences and needs of the carers was increased. The group also played a key role in the development of new community groups across a range of interests. This included the establishment of a Suraj arts group for the young adult children of carers and out of school provision for children with special needs.

Co-ordination

The group has been particularly successful at providing a voice for Asian women carers, whose confidence has grown both individually and collectively. Many now participate in other community activities including leisure and health classes. At the end of the project, this culminated in a presentation by representatives of the carers' group to the Deputy Director of Social Work leading to an invitation to submit proposals for funding for a carers' support project in the area. The increased confidence of the carers was noted both by them and other workers – 'Before I came to the group I didn't know what a social worker was. I'm now willing to challenge social workers' (Carer); 'Carers started to ask: "how many times are you going to ask us and not do anything?"' (Community Worker referring to consultation).

In response to carers' expressed needs, the weekly meetings of the group developed a stronger focus on social activity. Meanwhile, an area-wide Carers Forum is currently being developed that will have a more campaigning role.

In seeking to meet the needs of carers, social work and community work staff were given the opportunity to develop joint working between the council and voluntary agencies and, in so doing, to break down some of the professional and territorial barriers that had existed previously. Although there were some initial tensions in this process, relationships between staff groups in different agencies, as well as within the council, were strengthened and a spirit of collaboration encouraged. The result was the co-ordination of provision between a range of agencies. This not only maximised the use of resources but also led to joint training where staff were able to benefit from each other's skills and expertise. Looking at explanations for successes of the project, a middle manager referred particularly to 'openness to joint working by social work and voluntary sector staff'.

Need for bilingual staff
The communication networks with members of the minority ethnic communities were also improved and provided the basis for new areas of community work engagement. The experience of the work with carers informed the successful Ethnic Minority Social Inclusion Partnership bid for Glasgow, and this will provide opportunities for joint work with local communities in both East Pollokshields and Govanhill. Given the success of the community development process in working with carers in East Pollokshields, staff have agreed to renew work with carers in the Govanhill area, applying the lessons of the current work. As the social work area manager commented: 'we were previously struggling to meet the needs of Asian carers', indicating that there was a real sense of progress echoed by the carers themselves.

Throughout the project, a major issue has been the need for bilingual staff and advanced community work skills. Given the local staffing profile, this has involved a complex combination of inputs from the bilingual community work assistants and the qualified, but non-language-skilled, community workers. While all need-led practice must recognise the pace at which communities develop, the communication issues involved in this case were a significant influence on the pace and complexity of the development process. While ideally there would have been qualified bilingual staff, the practice illustrated that good progress can be made without the ideal resources. A senior manager referred to 'reflective practice and strategic links', a middle manager to 'well planned, sensitive and persistent community work practice', while a frontline agency worker noted that 'the language issues are very complex'.

South Lanarkshire

South Lanarkshire lies to the South of Glasgow and is a large local authority (population 300,0000) with three distinct but closely linked urban centres: Hamilton, the former new town of East Kilbride and Rutherglen/Cambuslang, both formerly part the city of Glasgow. There is also a large rural hinterland including several small towns and some quite remote and isolated villages.

Similar to Fife Council, a significant feature of South Lanarkshire was its development of a corporate strategy for social and economic development entitled 'Access and Opportunity', which emphasised citizen participation and involvement. It stated as its overall aim:

> *South Lanarkshire Council will work in partnership to build a competitive economy, realise the full potential of its resources and overcome disadvantage within its communities. It will extend access and opportunity and enhance the quality of life for all.*

Within this, it included disability, which was to become the focus of the project, and its consequences for social exclusion, alongside race, as one of the two key equal opportunity issues to be addressed.

Citizenship model

The project in South Lanarkshire was authority-wide. It focused on the participation of representatives of organisations of disabled people, or their carers, in a strategic approach to more responsive policy and practice by the council and other agencies over which it has an influence. Reflecting principles of the 'Access and Opportunity' strategy, the emphasis was on a citizenship model that focused on equality of access and opportunity for disabled people across all public services rather than just those with a specific remit to respond to disability. This point was emphasised by senior officers of the Social Work Department, who were the initial access point to the council, and reflected in the fact that the project related primarily to the Equal Opportunities rather than the Social Work Committee of the council.

Preliminary contact with the Social Work Department identified disability as a particular interest for the council, and it was agreed that a project might be developed to 'improve the way in which disabled people participate in and influence decisions about current services and plans for their future delivery'. The potential project was then discussed with two user and carer organisations – Hamilton and East Kilbride Disability Forum and Hamilton Community Care Forum. Initial reaction to the proposal was cautious. The organisations, particularly the disability forum, were concerned to ensure that involvement in the project would be in their interests and that it would be genuinely committed to participation and influence. Though fully committing themselves to involvement, this caution remained a feature of their engagement with the project.

Steering group

The project developed a strategy steering group of around 20 people consisting equally of officers of South Lanarkshire Council, from a range of departments, and members of disability and carer organisations. The steering group met bi-monthly as a full group with a variety of sub-groups developing work in relation to particular parts of the strategy. The first meeting confirmed the objective of the project as: 'To develop a user-led strategy for more responsive policies and services for disabled people in South Lanarkshire.' This was further elaborated with the following goals:

> *To influence each department of the council to develop its understanding of disability; to increase the involvement of disabled people in the design of policy; to develop service guidelines with real influence on practice by council departments.*

Initially, there was some frustration on the part of the disability organisations about the level of authority of the officers attending and their capacity to act on issues raised. Following intervention by the action-research team, the Head of Strategic Services in the Social Work Department agreed to take the chair on an interim basis with a commitment to transfer responsibility to a service user within six months. At the suggestion of the disability organisations, he later took on a joint chairing function with a service user. This 'committed, enthusiastic and positive joint leadership' (Agency Worker) was seen as a basis of the success of the project. At this stage, he also drew in the Head of Support Services (Leisure, Libraries and Cultural Services), who had become convenor of a recently established cross-departmental officer working group on disability, also reporting to the Equal Opportunities Committee. The status and authority of these officers, their strong commitment to community participation and their connections to key council committees were to be of great importance for the progress of the strategy group.

At the outset, disability activists suggested that images and perceptions of disability often did not relate to the reality of people's experience, with the result that council actions often failed to relate to needs effectively. Sometimes there was just a lack of awareness, and hence there was inaction. As one Head of Service in the council put it at the end of the project, a key lesson was: 'To stop the council "doing good" on behalf of others without checking out with users and carers their perspective – for us to get a healthy dose of reality from them.'

Agenda for action

Overall, where responses were made, they tended to be *ad hoc* when what was needed was a coherent strategy for inclusion of disabled people covering all areas of policy and practice. In reviewing their own performance, council officers acknowledged that there was much room for progress. Lack of disability awareness among many staff was acknowledged, consultation procedures, for example, in community care, were not necessarily effective in involving disabled people, housing stock adaptations had often led to segregation of disabled people, many council premises were not readily accessible. This openness about weaknesses in the council, and the recognition that they had much to learn from disabled people, facilitated the development of the partnership. It led on to a joint workshop between members of the strategy group to identify what could be achieved, the time scales for tackling particular issues, what the barriers might be and what strategies might be needed to overcome these.

A range of issues were highlighted in the workshop: the need to engage the participation of people across the full range of impairments; the need to move from reactive consultation with users to 'active forms of involvement in which people share in formulating policies rather than just responding to proposals'; the need to develop a checklist for monitoring the progress of council departments in considering and dealing with issues which are important to disabled people; the need to improve networking and joint action between disability organisations and council departments; the need for better information and training about disability; the need to resource an independent voice for disabled people through development of a centre for independent living.

From these issues the strategy group identified an agenda for action that has informed most of the subsequent work of the group. The key actions were to:

- respond to the draft strategic policy document 'Access and Opportunity'

- develop a good practice checklist in relation to disability to inform all service development and against which performance could be monitored and evaluated

- encourage the council to use the checklist in relation to contract specification with external agencies

- involve disability organisations on the steering group in provision of disability equality training for the council

- consider the development of a pilot training package on disability awareness for schools (subsequently this led on to a decision to establish a resource bank of training materials in the council)

- involve disabled people in an audit of needs and good and bad practice drawing on the checklist above

- review council employment practices and ensure that the 'double tick' standard was being met

- draw together a comprehensive list of agencies involved with disability in South Lanarkshire

- develop close working relationships with the Disability Officer group of the council and undertake joint training

- consider how to sustain the long-term development of the group, including consideration of a 'standing conference' on disability.

(Although it did not appear on the action list, the vision of a centre for independent living remained an important, though unfulfilled, goal for the disability activists.)

Benefits of participation

This list subsequently formed the core agenda of meetings. A work plan was developed from it, specifying key tasks, who would be responsible for progressing these, which other partners would be involved, the timescale for action and the resource implications. Progress against this work plan has been reviewed at each subsequent meeting and progress has been made on most aspects of the agenda. Of most influence has been the development and publication of the checklist of good practice in relation to disability. This has been influential well beyond South Lanarkshire but, within the project, it has been important in providing a platform for seeking to influence a range of council and related policies including, for example, 'Access and Opportunity', 'Hamilton Ahead' (the redevelopment programme for Hamilton town centre), community care plans, applications for planning and building control regulations.

Overall, community representatives felt they had been able to influence the council at a range of levels, well beyond those conventionally associated with community care, for example through quarterly meetings with Technical Services staff to consider aspects of planning and building warrant applications. They had also gained greater understanding of how policy was formed and finance allocated. Two comments from disability activists highlight their view of achievements: 'Getting across to council policy makers and learning to work comfortably and creatively together'; 'Establishing trust, turning officers who were reluctant (and on occasions hostile) around'.

Council officers recognised that the partnership was creating a more responsive approach to policy and practice and that it had shifted views on working with local people: 'Because of our contact with disabled people, the design process now feels real' (Service Head). The design of a successful bid by the council to participate in the 'Better Government for Older People' programme was acknowledged, for example, to have been built on the model established by the disability project. A specific initiative 'Access your Vote' was seen as: ' a very practical application of policy – big results at low cost'. One officer said at the end of the project: 'There's a lot of professional elitism around, particularly with technical staff, but I've noticed a definite shift in attitudes since we've been working with the group ...'

Mixed experiences

Neither council officers nor activists took the participation of the other for granted. Officers were particularly complimentary about the commitment of the activists: 'Amazing – they are a real asset to the groups they represent'; 'Puts the rest of us to shame'. Significant efforts were made to build a positive working relationship, for example, by the organisation of mutual training events, sharing information and by developing working relationships between the strategy group, the officers working group on disability and the council employees disability forum. Both the latter groups recognised that the understanding established between them in the group had not necessarily penetrated council services as extensively as they might have wished.

Disability organisations were sometimes highly critical of the performance of other parts of the council. For example, they felt that the Adult Care section of the Social Work Department was resisting exploration of the potential development of an independent living centre, describing their attitude as 'dictatorial', and a key officer responsible for consultation on the 'Access and Opportunity' strategy had been unresponsive. This frustration was not restricted to the community leaders. One officer, for example, reported at the end of the project: 'My work with the group does not even feature on my work programme, that's how important my manager sees it – so I have to find time outwith my agreed workload.'

There was, then, a degree of organisational ambivalence towards participation but, overall, there was a strong sense that the collaboration between officers and community leaders had been empowering to both parties in promoting change which reflected a citizenship and inclusion, rather than a service delivery perspective on disability. In the final questionnaires, officers and activists who were directly involved in the group commented very positively about one another. An agency worker talked of 'the high level of commitment from users and carers representatives', another of 'a growing trust and confidence amongst the participants'. Meanwhile, one activist talked of 'commitment and better understanding from policy makers', another referred to 'better interworking skills, e.g. listening and finding solutions' and another to 'being able to help shape policy and to feel you are being listened to and valued'.

Overall the project was felt to be successful. An agency worker, for example, talked of 'improved understanding of the benefits of involving users in policy and service design, particularly at the early stages – real partnership in planning', another of the value of 'new contacts, improved networking, advice and a different perspective'. The skills of all participants were felt to have been enhanced.

Comments from activists included:

Having a wider perspective on disability and how it impacts on everyone in the community.

My problem solving is more rational.

Gained confidence in the ability to influence partners.

Officers commented:

We no longer rely on technical manuals.

I have gained a lot personally from participation.

All our frontline staff now get disability awareness training. We are also looking to see if we can put something in our induction packs. Disability training will be part of the management foundation training programme (800 managers) and we are proposing that it will be compulsory for all recruitment panel chairs.

Lochaber, Highland

Lochaber is a large, and often remote, rural area in the west highlands of Scotland. It is part of the Highland Council area and centres on the town of Fort William. The town is an administrative centre for statutory and voluntary agencies serving the area, but the headquarters of most services are located on the opposite coast in Inverness, 65 miles away. While Fort William is an administrative focus, it, in turn, is as distant and, given the mountainous terrain, indented coastline, lack of public transport and rural road network, much more remote from many of the local communities it serves. A community worker commented: 'To get to one meeting, I set off at 8.30 and spent two hours on a chartered boat. I had to spend the night to get the next boat back and if the weather had turned I could have been there for days!' Remoteness and isolation of many communities are reinforced, especially in winter, by the weather conditions. Most of the settlements are very small, sometimes with fewer than 50 residents and never more than 1,000. They were described by one local worker as 'distinct and distinctive', while another emphasised 'people's commitment to the place they live in'.

The settlements are often widely spread and frequently have severely limited access to local services. The population is more mixed than might be anticipated. There is a long-standing, stable, local population, though younger people have sometimes felt obliged to move to seek employment opportunities. However, the area has also attracted incomers from other parts of Scotland and the UK. Differences in culture are sometimes a source of community tension. As a 91-year-old service user commented: 'I'm an incomer and integrating us with old time villagers has to be handled sensitively.' English is the predominant language, although, particularly in the west of the area, Gaelic is also spoken. Nonetheless, as a local worker commented: 'The make-up of the communities is strong because of historical links such as the church, crofting, fishing; generally people do not move away and have "memories" going back generations.'

It was these remote rural communities, rather than Fort William, which were the focus for the project. As with many other services, remote rural communities present particular problems for both the providers and the recipients of community care. These problems relate not only to service access but also to how user participation in service planning and delivery can be effectively and efficiently promoted. The project was concerned with both of these aspects of community care. However, as with other projects, it became increasingly apparent that community care concerns were only a sub-set of a wider range of issues affecting the health of communities and hence their capacity to provide a caring environment. A volunteer commented: 'I don't think it's just about community care – it's about isolated individuals' while a senior health service manager noted: 'Social isolation, deprivation and lack of transport are all things that have an impact on health.'

Intermediaries

The project was known as Rural Links and developed by Voluntary Action Lochaber (the local council for voluntary service) and Lochaber Community Care Forum, from an idea promoted by the Citizens' Advice Bureau. They had developed the concept of 'helplinks' to distribute CAB information. However, the Rural Links network envisaged a much more expansive role for volunteers. It would move well beyond the distribution of information for a single agency and 'Seek real community involvement in care issues with feedback to us as well as information distribution' (Voluntary Action Lochaber manager).

Volunteers

The Rural Links project focused on the recruitment of volunteers in the remote rural settlements of Lochaber. They would act both as intermediaries between service providers and users of community care and as a mutually supportive network which could draw on local experience and concerns of users and carers to inform the development of policy and practice. It was not seen as a substitute for direct user involvement but a way of facilitating communication and developing more responsive services. Highland Council and Highland Health Board were interested in reshaping community care joint planning arrangements and saw the links as a way of exploring a more participative approach. The action-research team became aware of the project as it was developing and, following local discussion, became involved in it.

Initial funding for the project came from the Scottish Office Rural Partnership Fund and support was provided by both Highland Council Social Work Department and Highland Health Board who were active partners in the project and its steering group. This funding enabled the recruitment and support of volunteers through a part-time co-ordinator. Subsequently, a successful application for funding from the National Lotteries Charities Board was made, enabling full-time employment of the co-ordinator for three years and four local, unqualified community workers on a one-day per week basis for two years.

The role of the community workers was to support the project in local communities and widen its scope beyond community care to issues such as rural transport, village halls, housing, community surveys and needs of young people. Additional funding from the action-research project enabled a fifth community worker to be appointed on the same basis for one year but with a specific focus on community care. (While initially unqualified, during their employment, arrangements were made for the community workers to attend an outreach Higher Certificate in Community Work Course run by Glasgow University Department of Adult and Continuing Education. Several Rural Link volunteers also completed this course.)

Although levels of activity varied, by July 1997, 80 Rural Link volunteers were registered with the project. Sixty of these attended a conference in November that year, representing 15 different rural communities and 19 local voluntary groups. From the initial recruitment phase, the emphasis was less on extending the number of volunteers and more on supporting them to offer a quality service.

Local networks

Approximately half the Links were people with a professional role and interest in community care, such as GPs and health visitors, who took the work on as an additional but related task. The other half constituted a cross-section of local people, mainly women, with an interest in community care, either because they used services, or because they were active in other local community groups and voluntary organisations, including churches and community councils. The Links were characterised by the fact that they were clearly established in local networks and community developments. One agency worker described them as 'the eyes and ears of the community'. Another commented: 'The main benefit of Rural Links is their acceptability to local people as a conduit for information – local messengers are trusted'. Rural Links described their ideal characteristics as 'knowledgeable', 'trustworthy', 'persistent', 'gatherers of information' and 'great at listening'. Another key feature was localness. As one commented: 'Communities respond best to one of their own', and another: 'We're a "kent face" that is trusted to take care of people's feelings.'

Development of services

Voluntary Action Lochaber prepared a directory of information resources about a wide range of services relevant to community care that was a core resource for Links to use. They also took responsibility for making it available in as many public places as possible. An agency worker described the most important outcome of the project as an 'established network which can be used to push information or draw it in'. The senior social work manager commented: 'On the whole people now know who's who and who does what', but noted that health agencies were an exception.

Through the Rural Links, not only were the statutory providers able to pass on and receive information, but a range of smaller voluntary agencies were better able to offer a service in Lochaber – these included Alzheimers Scotland, the Red Cross, the Chest and Stroke Association and Age Concern (the local organiser of which was a significant contributor to the development of the project and its steering group). A senior agency manager commented: 'Most voluntary sector organisations were very involved and made good use of the network of links.'

The employment from the beginning of 1999 of the part-time (one day per week) community workers had advanced the development of the project though the level of focus on community care issues varied from worker to worker. The worker whose post was funded for a year from the action-research project was able to focus specifically on care needs. The potential of the approach is well illustrated by the kind of activity that a very small investment can make in mobilising voluntary effort and responding to care needs in a remote community – in this case Nether Lochaber, Kinlochleven, Ballachullish, Glencoe, Duror and Ardgour.

A local network of Rural Links was supported through bimonthly meetings, five new Links being recruited during the year. The worker and group members responded to a range of needs in the community including:

- accessing music therapy for a disabled child

- engaging voluntary visitors to support an overstretched carer

- providing information about services

- extending the Highland Help Call checks to Glencoe

- providing support to a young mother who had had a stroke

- referring volunteers to a placement agency

- acting as an advocate for a service user in relation to Occupational Therapy

- working on development of a community car scheme to help people to get to services

- setting up and supporting a monthly afternoon club for older people

- setting up and supporting assisted shopping trips using a community minibus

- undertaking a survey of home support needs.

The worker also acted as a link with statutory providers and voluntary agencies, both referring individuals and receiving requests for assistance. She was invited to discuss issues affecting the local community with statutory providers. For example, having consulted with Rural Links and through them with service users, she met with the area social work manager to discuss the future development of residential services for older people.

Change in relationships

The illustration of work in one community provides an insight into the very practical contribution that the Rural Links scheme has made. These practical results were seen by participants at the final review of the project as key achievements. But behind the practical was a sense of significant change in relationships between service users and providers. Community volunteers were seen as genuine partners and there was a belief that the voice of users and carers had been significantly enhanced. The senior social work manager, commenting on trends in community care, said:

Complex care assessments have become budget and 'client' driven. We talk in a language of care management and have lost sight of the rounded social worker. We need to broaden care management out to include anyone and everyone that has an involvement.

In this context, the following comments are pertinent: one agency worker talked of 'Rural Links being accepted by professional agencies', another of 'growing confidence among the community that they can make things happen'. One community worker said:

'Links see they can make a difference' and another: 'Social Work management are willing to be held to account now.'

Project participants welcomed the level of activity generated by the Rural Links initiative but also acknowledged a number of limitations to the work. The response from professional agencies on the ground was patchy. This was primarily related to certain local agencies that saw the work of the project as peripheral. One Rural Link stated:

> They see us as amateurs. It's not until we prove that we are relevant that they sit up and take notice. You can get a health visitor who is great in one village and in the next her colleague doesn't want to know. It's the same with Social Work and with GPs. You can't predict it.

Despite such experiences, a new joint planning structure for the Lochaber area is under consideration, with voluntary and community organisations playing a stronger role as more equal partners in the process. Participants reported a significant shift in the quality of inter-agency relationships related to the experience of the Rural Links project and commended Social Work services on their alternative approaches to care planning consultation. A voluntary agency worker commented that the Social Work Department 'has made real inroads into involving users and carers in the planning process for community care', and the senior social work manager commented: 'Attitudes have changed – staff now value the opinions of local people.'

Rural Links became involved in a variety of community care strategy groups in partnership with users and carers, advocating on behalf of local users and communities. However, their primary value has been in supporting a network of effective communications. One agency worker commented on the value of 'using very local people as "messengers" – because it increases local knowledge and skills, its non-threatening and promotes ownership of the information'. The contribution of the Links was recognised as varying between individuals but described by one agency manager as 'in many cases beyond the call of duty'.

3 Themes and issues

Policy and strategy context

The projects described in the previous section all provide evidence of the benefits that community development approaches can offer in the context of community care. The approach is not presented in any sense as a panacea, but its potential has been largely neglected. We were aware that there were already projects in community care that were adopting community development. However, most of these were isolated initiatives that were not necessarily embedded in the normal policy and practice of similar agencies whether public, voluntary, community or private sector. Our objective, through this action-research, was to look in more depth at what the issues would be within mainstream agencies. While each of the projects has characteristics that are unique to its own context, they illustrate a range of initiatives that could be highly relevant in many other localities. Community development is an organic process that must embrace local history, perspectives, aspirations and culture. Hence the case studies are not presented as models for direct replication. Nonetheless, they provide many lessons that are universally relevant.

Embarking on this study in 1997, we did not anticipate the degree to which the policy context of the projects, in terms of social inclusion and social justice, would impact on their development, nor did we anticipate the significance of the 'modernising government' debate. Both became the backcloth against which the project was conducted. The former provided direct encouragement to progressive local authorities to develop explicit commitments to more inclusive policies and practice. Examples, such as the Fife 'Citizenship Commission' or the South Lanarkshire 'Access and Opportunity' policy, are illustrative. The latter was potentially more contradictory, introducing greater commitment to community participation, consultation and decentralisation simultaneously with a stronger emphasis on target setting and performance monitoring.

This tension is well illustrated in the policy of 'Best Value' that both encourages user voice and requires performance review against explicit criteria. Whether there is incompatibility depends on whether the criteria for measurement are a product of participative governance or professional or political prescription. In the four projects, increasing influence of the 'new managerialism', reflected in major restructuring of the local authorities in which they operated, sometimes sat uneasily alongside an aspiration to more responsive and participative local governance.

Policy context

None of this context was unique to the project sites – it is characteristic of the national policy and practice climate. It can be illustrated in the specific policies for community care and the broader policies for development of local government and its relationship with the community and other potential partners. For example, the first line of the 1999 White Paper *Aiming for Excellence – Modernising Social Work Services in Scotland* reads: 'People who use the services have clear views of what social work services should be ...' Its first objective is: 'To involve people who need care, and those who care for them, in planning services ...'

The theme of community involvement had been developed more fully in relation to community care in the 1998 Scottish Office paper *Modernising Community Care*:

New local partnerships may be necessary, not just between social work, health and housing agencies, but also with:

- *education, leisure and recreation;*

- *independent community care providers; and*

- *people using services locally.*

These partnerships ... should develop to reflect the needs of the area. It is most important to involve the people using the services and their carers ... This more local approach offers considerable scope to work more effectively in partnership with people who use services, rather than doing things to them. The result should be communities which are more involved, helped and supported by community care.

Meanwhile in its 1997 *Millennium Report*, the Association of Directors of Social Work in Scotland stated that a community development approach is 'a central strategy for local authorities and other agencies' and concluded that it would 'help users, carers and the wider community to: participate in the planning of social services; influence the delivery of social work services; where appropriate, provide social work services.'

More broadly these statements of principle were consistent with the overall strategy of government to promote social inclusion and encourage community participation. The former is illustrated in the 1999 Scottish Executive paper, *Social Inclusion: Opening the Door to a Better Scotland*, which states that: [Empowerment is] 'a principle underlying the Government's approach' and that: 'A long term difference will be most likely if action is based on the principle of handing over power to individuals and communities'. The latter is reflected in the Convention of Scottish Local Authorities and Scottish Office consultative paper on community planning (1998), which identified the following objective:

To provide a process through which councils and their public sector partners, in consultation with the voluntary and the private sector, and the community, can agree both a strategic vision for the area and the action which each of the partners will take in pursuit of that vision.

Ironically then, despite the relative infrequency of good examples of practice in relation to community care, the policy framework in Scotland was explicitly encouraging the kind of approach that the four projects were adopting. This would also have been true if the projects had been located elsewhere in the UK. Yet a positive policy climate was not enough to ensure effective development. There were the countervailing influences of the 'new managerialism' and restructuring to contend with and a broader concern about a potential contradiction between policy intent and the established culture and behaviour of local government. As a recent Joseph Rowntree Foundation report, exploring the situation in English local authorities, concluded:

> *Developing a stronger relationship with its public is central to local government's future. Tackling many of the issues confronting local authorities requires the involvement and ideas of local people and government structures which are in touch with the public's varying views and needs ... The agenda of change ... will require massive changes to the culture, role and structure of the political and managerial arrangements of the council.* (Filkin *et al.*, 1999)

It is in the context of the need to achieve 'massive changes' that the micro-level experience of the four projects may offer some insights. The policies frequently refer to the importance of partnerships and the idea that different partners are stakeholders with interests that need to be acknowledged. With this in mind, we now focus on the central issues that the projects have highlighted in relation to four active stakeholders in the four sites – community leaders, service users, frontline workers and managers. (It should be noted that politicians were generally not directly active in the projects.) In summarising the perspectives, we have sought to relate the statements and comments of stakeholders to the wider policy context.

Community leaders

The community leaders in all the sites were involved entirely voluntarily – as members of community groups, user groups and as volunteers. Their motivation to become and stay involved related strongly to their judgements of the costs and benefits of engagement with the project. Since the agencies in all sites were committed to implementing policies that valued community participation, there was a real sense in which community leaders could employ resource power by deciding to engage with or withdraw from projects. This is illustrated by the example of the disability organisations in South Lanarkshire. If pursued, their non-cooperation could have rendered inoperable the aspiration to policies based on participation and partnership. In this context, the community leaders were not, therefore, simply supplicants seeking a place at the table but, if the practice was to live up to its rhetoric, an essential component for the approach. This is increasingly the case as public policy is formulated within the 'modernising government' agenda that promotes more participative concepts of democracy. Community organisations have enhanced bargaining power.

In the projects, the community leaders demonstrated this potential in three ways:

- as conduits for ideas, passing them on to other members and to council officers

- as convenors, pulling ideas together, playing a clear leadership role

- as catalysts – being prepared to start new initiatives or embrace new ideas.

In working in these ways, community leaders displayed the following characteristics:

- a high level of commitment to ensuring that the goals of the groups were achieved

- perseverance and resilience, often in the face of disappointments and frustrations

- skills of working within group situations and in building relationships with a wide range of professional practitioners and managers

- awareness that they needed to relate to a broader constituency than just the members of a small group

- ability to see the bigger picture, especially the constraints under which local authorities have to operate as a result of government policies and reduced resources.

In relation to these characteristics, it is important to note that volunteer community leaders demonstrated skills that frequently paralleled those of the agency staff. For example, the disability activists in South Lanarkshire had executive and management responsibilities for local organisations including employment of staff, and in Lochaber Rural Link volunteers were engaged in professional training alongside the local community workers.

Commitment

Community leaders were reflective about the commitment that their involvement required. In South Lanarkshire, one commented: 'It takes a long time to be able to meet each others needs and see tangible results.' Another noted: 'The biggest commitment is time.'

Other stakeholders were consistently positive about the commitment of community leaders and sometimes appeared quite surprised by the benefits that had come from partnership working. A frontline worker in South Lanarkshire noted 'the high level of commitment from users and carers representatives – a lot of work done behind the scenes.' Another welcomed 'making contact with such enthusiastic, positive and committed people.' An agency worker in Fife commented on 'the commitment by several individuals active in the community to ensure and facilitate ongoing dialogue with the community.' Another noted how 'the core group of volunteers has been extremely committed to the project'. A senior manager in Glasgow referred to the value of 'long-standing relationships with well developed community networks'.

A frequently posed question in community development is what motivates people to become so involved, to give considerable amounts of time voluntarily – self-interest, altruism or a combination of both? It is impossible to give a clear answer, but certainly, in all four sites, evidence of altruism – genuine concern for the situation of other people – was clearly present. But it is important to recognise too that many of the community leaders were members of the community which could benefit from changes made. Community leaders also valued their own development and the capacity for effective action built by their organisations. One referred to gaining 'confidence in the ability to influence partners', another to 'being accepted by professional agencies'. Other stakeholders observed the same development, noting, for example, 'growing confidence among the community that they can make things happen' and 'increased confidence of individual volunteers in their ability to make things happen'.

Trust and personal authority

Interestingly in none of the projects was there a mass base of community opinion that was mobilised by the community leaders. Although there are methods such as citizen or user panels which can widen participation, there was little evidence that such approaches would have been seen as beneficial to the particular objectives of the projects. The influence exerted by the activists in the projects does not, therefore, rest on real capacity to mobilise community support, and hence apply coercive power, but on an acceptance by the holders of key resources that the views presented could be regarded as accurate reflections of broader concerns and priorities. An activist in South Lanarkshire stated that an important outcome from the project was, 'being able to help shape policy and feel that you are being listened to and valued'.

There was, therefore, a key element of trust among the officers about the genuineness and accuracy of the community perspective being presented by a relatively small number of community leaders. In South Lanarkshire in particular, the need to build a stronger base of active community support was a continuing concern of the disability activists.

Some community leaders were particularly influential as a result of personal authority resting in their recognised experience, commitment and ability. This was evident in all the projects in different ways. In South Lanarkshire, it was illustrated in the joint chairing of the strategy group between an officer and community leader. In South Lanarkshire, Lochaber and Fife, volunteers and community leaders were able to engage with a variety of agency staff. Long-standing records of service to their communities and a capacity to articulate community concerns were readily acknowledged by professionals. Similarly, the influence of the community leaders in the Glasgow project rested to a significant extent on their personal authority, arising from direct experience in carrying very demanding caring responsibilities.

Service users

The relationship of the project to service users was different in each project. It is difficult therefore to generalise from the experience. In

Glasgow, the Asian carers were direct recipients of services, though in an intermediary relationship between providers and the actual service users. While the beneficiary group was wider than just those who were active, they might best be described as a campaigning, self-help organisation of service users.

In South Lanarkshire, users and community leaders were synonymous. This model can perhaps be best described as a coalition of disability interests, entering into partnership with the council, operating from a tradition of both direct services and pressure group activity. But the community leaders were acting on behalf of a very large constituency, across the whole of the council area, with which it had limited direct contact. Most user beneficiaries were distant from the work of the community leaders. It is even questionable how far the intended beneficiaries were aware that the strategy group existed.

In Fife, as in South Lanarkshire, the community leaders had a long history of community involvement. Some would certainly be potential service users, but it was not this identity that seemed to inform their community involvement. Thus the users in Kincardine were largely distinct from the community leaders and came into contact with the project mainly through participation events and outreach work, including the community surveys and information provision.

In Lochaber, the distinction between community leaders/volunteers and users was evident. Rural Links clearly acted on behalf of users, though it is important to appreciate that some were service users and/or carers and therefore had first-hand experience of the issues involved in the project.

Active participants

There is therefore a blurred distinction between community leaders and users in all the projects: sometimes users are beneficiaries, sometimes they are participants in a project, and sometimes they are both. This illustrates the importance of developing initiatives with a flexible appreciation of the user/leader relationship and a recognition that being a potential or actual service user is not necessarily any impediment to being an effective community leader. Any suggestion that the term user might equate with the idea of dependence is firmly refuted by the experience of these projects. Users demonstrated their capacity to be active players in participative governance.

It is important too to be clear that the focus of their participation was not restricted to the specific services provided within community care. Their participation in these projects expressed a wider demand for issues to be addressed across a range of dimensions of their lives to enable full citizenship to be realised.

However, it is important also to acknowledge that not all users have the same capacity, opportunity or motivation to be active. Indeed the lack of a mass, active constituency of users in any of the projects suggests that it is realistic not to expect the number of people directly involved to be large. Such a conclusion would not be peculiar to community care; mass-based community involvement is generally rare.

It is also important to acknowledge that some underlying concerns in community care about the relationships between users and carers were to be found within the projects. In particular, the different perspectives of users and carers and whose voice should be most influential remains problematic. In the Glasgow project, for example, the primary focus to date has been on the voice of carers. They have their own needs but are also intermediaries between users and service providers. The issue of intermediary roles also arises, particularly in relation to the functions of Rural Links, though it was present too in South Lanarkshire and Fife. In South Lanarkshire, for example, disabled community leaders were sometimes engaged in discussions which related to services other than those of which they were direct users.

Users and leaders

All of the projects were sensitive to the issues relating to intermediary roles for community leaders and recognised the potential effects of the filtering of information. The fact that community leaders were themselves frequently service users was a significant strength but it does not remove the need for reflective practice and attention to validating perspectives from the direct experience of users.

Where they had a direct link to the projects, carers in the Glasgow and users in Fife and Lochaber frequently expressed their confidence and trust in community leaders/volunteers who were acting on their behalf. This required them to have good relationships with community leaders and vice versa, to see them as people who were really seeking to work for them.

This relationship could be observed by other stakeholders who could themselves then be confident of the role that community leaders were playing on behalf of users. One of the practitioners in Fife expressed this confidence by stating that the thing that enabled successful outcomes to happen was, 'The commitment by several individuals active in the community to ensure and facilitate ongoing dialogue with the community.' However, in South Lanarkshire, the situation was different. Here the direct relationship between leaders and users was conducted through the organisations from which the community leaders were drawn rather than through the project itself. The other stakeholders therefore had to trust that these relationships validated the stances that leaders adopted. Describing the sources of success in the project, one senior manager in South Lanarkshire pointed to 'a growing confidence and trust amongst the participants'.

Frontline workers

There is evidence from each of the projects of the advantages to be gained from practitioners' being highly accessible to community members. It meant that rapid, direct communication was possible and that mutual trust could be developed. This finding echoes community development experience more generally: the ability of local people to have contact, on a day-to-day basis, with a practitioner – and vice versa – is known to make sense.

Also of central importance in the projects was the style adopted by frontline workers and the language they used when working with local people. On both counts the emphasis was on accessibility – demonstrating to those around them their commitment to providing support and their willingness to listen to the opinions of local people and act on them. There is clear evidence from the projects that having the services of skilled and committed practitioners 'on the ground' paid enormous dividends. They were able to encourage activists to be confident about their plans, they provided continuity over a period of two or three years, and they helped connect the concerns of local communities with the decision-making processes of local authorities.

Work with communities

A key group of workers in the projects were community workers. Explaining the success of the project, a middle manager in Glasgow Social Work Department talked of 'skilled and well supported community work input sustained over a substantial period'. A senior manager in Lochaber said: 'Community worker input has helped local people deal with meetings and conflict better.' A Rural Link in Lochaber said: 'We need skilled community workers with a generic remit, based much more locally.'

The case studies also indicate the importance of the community work skills of the user and carer support workers in South Lanarkshire and the key contribution made by the community social worker and community worker in Fife. The shift in practice culture to more direct engagement with communities and to partnership working was also required of other frontline staff. In Glasgow, a middle manager referred to the importance of 'openness to joint working by social work and voluntary sector staff'. An agency worker in South Lanarkshire stressed the value of 'improved understanding of the benefits of involving users in policy and service design, particularly at the early stages – real partnership in planning'. A senior manager in Corporate Resources in South Lanarkshire stated: 'We need skilled staff to help build the capacity of the voluntary sector.' A frontline social worker in Fife said: 'The high level of contact with local people has assisted in raising the profile of the enquiry information team and helped "demystify" social work.' A senior manager in the Social Work Department in Lochaber commented: 'Attitudes have changed – staff now value the opinions of local people.'

The emphasis given to accessibility and contact between frontline staff, service users and community organisations, particularly in social work departments, is a pertinent reminder of the degree to which recent trends in practice have moved away from earlier localisation and participatory principles. Ironically, at a time when the general policy climate is emphasising these principles, social work, with an emphasis on individual case management, seems to have lost touch with such roots. Yet if the aspiration to move from community care to caring communities is to be realised, the localisation and participatory principles are essential.

Personal authority

The competence of the workers is clearly a significant factor.
However, recognition of this factor by senior officers (and by other
participants) generates recognition of personal authority that
enhances scope for influence. This recognition is sometimes
described as referent authority in that it not only reflects the
characteristics of the individual but also their positive association
with more powerful players. Examples are evident in all the
projects:

- In Glasgow, the senior community worker and his team were
  able to develop work with the ethnic minority carers not only
  because it fulfilled statutory and policy objectives and because
  they were competent practitioners, but also because they had
  the support and confidence of the area social work manager.

- In Fife, it was some time before the project really took off. In
  part, this reflected a need on the part of the frontline workers to
  be confident that they would have the support of senior officers.
  Their influence grew perceptibly as the efforts to engage the
  local community became more imaginative and more
  successful. The recognition of their competence gave them a
  leadership role in the project that belied their formal status.

- The local community workers employed by Voluntary Action
  Lochaber were of junior status in conventional bureaucratic
  terms being both part-time and, initially, unqualified. Yet with a
  history of involvement in local community affairs, sound local
  knowledge and networks, evident enthusiasm and commitment,
  they were able to become significant intermediaries.

There was a symbiosis between frontline workers and senior
managers in the projects which was of considerable significance for
the action-research. Through providing support for frontline
workers, senior managers could play a significant role in the local

projects. Equally, the work of frontline staff contributed to the strategic function of the local authorities.

Not surprisingly, everything was not all sweetness and light: there were instances of contradictions between stated intentions to promote participation and the manner in which agencies approached the task. For example, when the Social Work Department in Fife first consulted with the local community about the community care plan, it did so in a relatively formal manner, sending out full copies of a lengthy and complex plan written primarily for a professional audience, inviting community representatives to a meeting to hear a verbal presentation about it and pass on comments. The workers were conscious that this was not a good approach but, constrained by time and resources, they felt unable, in the short term, to proceed in any other way. The result was complaints about lack of clarity and specificity in relation to the needs of the locality. To the credit of the Social Work staff involved, they were self-critical and recognised the gap between their aspirations and their practice. As the project developed more collaborative relationships with local people, the effort put into more imaginative forms of participation paid dividends. Isolating community care from other community issues was recognised as inappropriate from a community perspective.

Managers

One respondent to the end of project questionnaire, when commenting on the positive aspects of the action-research in relation to the local authority, states that the council is 'now more likely to have a dialogue about common issues and view matters less departmentally'. It is a comment that mirrors the aspirations of national policymakers for 'joined-up' government, and it is a comment which illustrates the expectations being placed on local authority managers to respond to three imperatives:

- to work corporately within the local authority, not departmentally

- to work jointly with other statutory organisations, the private sector and with voluntary organisations

- to find ways of increasing the participation of citizens – local governance rather than local government.

These agenda items were recognised by managers as presenting a major challenge and requiring a change of mind-set both by senior and middle managers:

We no longer feel we can develop policy in isolation. (Executive Director, Education Resources, South Lanarkshire)

The work forced me to review my practice. (Senior Manager, Glasgow Social Work Department)

Some parts of the service need to make dialogue with service users/carers/activists a more natural and endemic activity. (Senior Manager, Fife Social Work Department)

The willingness of agencies to look at new ways of working. (Senior manager, Highland Social Work Department)

We no longer rely on formal technical manuals to guide our work – we now ask users and try to compromise on the various needs of different disabilities. (Head of Technical Services, Housing and Technical Resources, South Lanarkshire)

New structures and roles

As well as requiring managers to rethink their approach within their organisation, towards other organisations and to the community, the challenge also implies the need for important shifts in the way that strategies for practice are designed and developed and the way that work and staff are organised. A participative approach to governance requires responsiveness from managers whose task is to develop service responses in partnership with others in the light of the particular needs, experiences and resources of specific communities. While there must be continual attention to equity between localities in the allocation of resources, it is an approach that militates against uniformity and standardisation of service provision. New structures, engaging other provider partners and the community, are needed in order to respond to a new managerial remit.

In this context, a key organisational change identified in the action-research was the removal of a rigorous distinction, in practice, between strategic and operational management: no longer can one group of senior managers concern themselves only with the first, isolated from the more practical aspects associated with the second – and vice versa. Managers have to do both.

Ability and commitment

In all of the projects, officers of local government have been significant players. The statutory and policy frameworks within which they are employed legitimised their use of power to particular ends. They were able to play a role which went some way towards fulfilling the aspirations of corporate policies relating to such themes as decentralisation and community participation. They were also able to embed their stances in the obligations of their agencies to statutes relating not only to community care but also to areas such as housing, planning and building control or disability rights. At the same time, they were unable to follow through options that were beyond their authority.

Yet the influence of senior officers did not rest solely on their bureaucratic authority. There are two main reasons for this. First, in partnerships of the kind illustrated in this study, such officers also have to be convincing to community activists, to their peers in other departments and to other agencies over which they exercise no formal power. Secondly, to achieve their ends, they are also dependent on the performance of their subordinates whose motivation and commitment is related to the conditions under which they are required to work.

There are good illustrations from the projects of the use by senior officers of personal authority and charisma to motivate and secure the involvement of those over whom they did not have authority. Community leaders in particular commented directly on the performance of key officers, and it is clear that partnerships were often sustained only because there was confidence in their demonstrated ability and commitment. Equally, there were many illustrations of the dependence of strategic staff on the competence of operational staff.

In South Lanarkshire, for example, community leaders were reluctant at first to enter into a partnership with the council. This judgement was based on previous poor experience of council officers. Their commitment could not be secured solely by demonstration of goodwill by council officers, it also required evidence that officers' performance would help the activists accomplish their objectives. That the partnership flourished was in large part a product of the recognition by key officers that their capacity to be influential could not rest on bureaucratic status. It is important to emphasise how the research evidence points to the need for senior managers to become actively involved in partnership work. It cannot be left to middle managers.

Minimal Health Board involvement

A perceived weakness of all the projects, though significantly less pronounced in Lochaber, was the failure to engage the involvement of health agencies adequately. Part of the explanation for this is to be found in power relationships. In South Lanarkshire, Glasgow and Fife, attempts were made by senior officers to engage the relevant Health Boards and other health agencies but, while there were positive individual participants such as a health visitor in Fife, institutionally they largely ignored overtures to become involved. The positive relationship enjoyed between the Social Work Department, the Health Board and the voluntary agency in Lochaber was largely based on the shared values and objectives of key staff but did not extend effectively to the local Health Trust.

The consistent difficulty in engaging health agencies is of considerable concern in the context of the emphasis of current policy on partnership and participation to produce improved health outcomes. The lesson to be drawn from the low-level involvement of health organisations in the action-research is twofold. There needs to be deliberate and sustained work by senior managers in the lead agency to make links with other organisations and ensure that shared values inform the coming together. Equally, on this evidence, the health sector needs to address the growing gap between its policy rhetoric and its practice performance. Without these the necessary conditions for the building of effective partnership working cannot be established.

A key theme running through the approach of all four stakeholders is that of trust. It is a key commodity for effective projects. It needs to exist at a variety of levels: between managers, workers and community leaders and between community leaders and service users. As an Age Concern worker in Lochaber put it: 'The main benefit of Rural Links is their acceptability to local people as a conduit of information. Local messengers are trusted.'

At a very practical level, the case studies show that community leaders working on behalf of users and supported by frontline workers and managers can promote tangible improvements in users' quality of life.

Implications

The four perspectives summarised above have significant implications for agency policies and strategies. Most prominent is the theme of interdependence. Each group of participants has a distinctive role to play, and it is critical that each one of them contributes. Change is unlikely to take place if only one or two of the players are involved – the process would be skewed or blocked. The connections between the various participants in community development and partnerships have to be strong, substantive and interactive. They can neither be nominal nor one way. This finding has profound implications for partnership work, especially in the context of regeneration and social inclusion.

The trust which was so evident in the projects was not unconditional. It rested on continued evidence that actions and words were consistent, that commitments were fulfilled. It could not rest on unrealistic expectations – all parties had to accept a range of constraints impinging on their partners. To push another partner too far would put a partnership at risk, undermine trust and hence the working relationships.

It would be incorrect to assume that mutual respect was a sufficient basis for sustaining the partnerships. Tangible progress that fulfilled the aspirations of each was also a necessary condition. Some participants withdrew or participated only at particular periods. The balance of costs and benefits appeared for them to shift while, for those retaining continuous involvement, the benefits outweighed the costs. Yet without the underlying search among all participants to sustain mutual trust, such calculations would not have been meaningful.

Making connections work effectively between people (community leaders and users), structures (principally, in these case studies, the local authority but potentially health agencies and others) and social policies (government) is a central responsibility for community development. It needs to be undertaken at different levels, notably the strategic and the operational, and both between organisations (partnerships) and within organisations (corporate policies).

The evidence of this study is that even those people or groups who are seen as relatively excluded, or of relatively low organisational status, have the capacity to exercise power. Power can be employed in a contest or it can be used to mutual benefit. For the most part, the projects have sought to maximise benefits by emphasising mutual interests.

4 Doing it in practice?

We have referred to the energy and commitment to be found in the projects, particularly among the volunteers and community leaders: 'Their commitment is amazing – they are a real asset to the groups they represent' (Agency Worker, South Lanarkshire). At the same time, each group of participants had a good understanding and appreciation of others' contributions.

The implication of the high level of activity and interactions between groups was that, on each site, the picture was a complex one. There was potential for misunderstanding and conflict within each project, yet generally these were overcome.

Every local authority and voluntary agency planning to develop the approach discussed in this report will face a similar situation: each community is different and unique and interventions have to take this into account. Yet, while there is no template, some basic ground rules can be identified from an analysis of the four projects. This enables us to set down the essential ingredients required for the successful development of caring communities.

Building on what exists

The approach taken in any one locality is dependent on what is there already – the character of the community, the history of community activities and action, strengths and weaknesses of voluntary and community organisations, the nature of informal networks and the presence of particular individuals. This is a lesson that statutory agencies seem to find difficult to learn because of the increasing dominance of output and target-led approaches in their programmes and services. As we noted earlier, what is needed is equity not uniformity of development. The need to prepare approaches to communities from a position of knowing what is there and deliberately building on it is very apparent from the projects.

Needs-led practice

Starting from what exists does not mean that approaches have to be unplanned – quite the opposite: a clear strategy is essential. It is precisely because the change process is complex that those responsible for community development programmes need to have clear goals and objectives. It means, however, that resources for investigating needs, and entering into dialogue with communities about them, have to be allocated in advance of planning any programme of action. Partnerships based on trust have to be built from shared perceptions of what needs to be done and how. It is not enough, therefore, to apply normative or comparative criteria to the assessment of need. To capture the motivation and the energy that communities can themselves bring, it is essential that felt needs are brought into expression and that the agenda for action addresses those things that are of real importance to the community.

The researchers were struck by the crucial role played by community workers in helping local people develop their agendas and build their organisations. Ensuring that there are resources for employing community development staff is essential. The action-research draws attention to the transferability of the community development process. Community workers can be located, therefore, in any one of a number of local authority departments.

Involving managers

It is essential to work out the best way to bring senior managers and politicians on board. Supportive managers are invaluable for frontline staff. Their involvement can lift the morale of all participants and can ease the process of accessing resources and information. Adequate time, as well as training opportunities, need to be made available for managers to play a substantive part in community-based approaches to social inclusion and caring communities.

While the action-research yielded only a small amount of data on the relationship between elected members of local authorities and community organisations, the need to involve politicians in the planning and to keep them informed of developments is essential.

Forming partnerships

As we have seen in these projects, community perceptions of need were much broader than those of specific agencies. To address them, extensive inter-agency and interdisciplinary practice, as well as community involvement, were necessary. Partnership was key, but no two local developments followed the same pattern. It is important, therefore, to think about how effective partnerships can be built: they need to be put together carefully, identifying which are the most appropriate community and professional organisations to be represented on them.

There can be no template for forming partnerships. They have to be created to fit particular community and organisational circumstances. Accordingly, we should expect to see a variety of different kinds of partnerships operating up and down the country. Partnerships will not be able to work effectively if they do not have legitimacy in the eyes of those on whose behalf they act. All stakeholders need to be engaged, from the start, in agreeing the terms of reference, structures and procedures. They also need to be engaged in continuous evaluation and learning from the experience in order to adjust and develop their performance effectively (Henderson and Mayo, 1998).

Social inclusion framework

Whatever the precise form of partnership, a strong, overarching value framework is essential. In the context of this study, the evidence is that the care needs of communities can be addressed best by being conceived and planned within a corporate, social inclusion framework rather than within the community care legislation. In local authorities, the issue of caring communities must form part of corporate policymaking rather than being left to the Social Work/Social Services Department. The promotion of caring communities is a task for everyone involved in community planning. Specific obligations in relation to provision of individual community care services, to which local authorities and health partners must respond, are only one dimension of a wider agenda within which the obligations should be placed.

This conclusion is consonant with the Government's insistence on 'joined up' thinking and action. Departmentalism is in the past, and neighbourhood management, within a social inclusion framework, is on the horizon. There is a realisation that a holistic and coordinated approach is required in order to respond to the economic, social and environmental needs of individuals and communities. To be genuinely inclusive, it must take account of the needs of all. Among the most disadvantaged are carers and care users whose circumstances often lead to exclusion and loss of opportunity for full citizenship. This is an issue of rights as well as services.

This study's finding is that community care practice and strategies need to relate to this new agenda, alongside other mainstream areas – housing, economic development, community safety etc. – not simply in terms of planning and delivering services, but as part of a clear commitment to supporting community involvement. As we have seen, these principles are already embedded in policy. Practice is lagging behind.

The action-research has demonstrated the paramount importance of ensuring that people retain their choice of which community or communities they wish to identify with. It is essential that the issue of user involvement is not simply encapsulated within the concept of social inclusion on the assumption that it will take place as part of a wider process of participation. On the contrary, because there is the risk of user involvement becoming 'lost' within social inclusion policies, and because many commissioners are still unaware of key aspects of facilitating user involvement (Joseph Rowntree Foundation, 1999), there is also a need to retain and improve existing, effective mechanisms for supporting user involvement.

Making use of community development

The core group of volunteers has been extremely committed to the project. When we talk about a team out here it comprises of workers and volunteers each looking out for the other and working in partnership to achieve aims.

This statement from a worker in Fife captures the idea of process which is at the heart of community development: cooperation and engagement by a range of groups and organisations – community and professional – in a shared endeavour. On numerous occasions the action-research provided examples of the need to have community development in order to strive for the goal of caring communities. Sometimes, it is expressed through a practitioner's skills, sometimes by the intervention of a senior local authority manager and sometimes by the actions of users and community members. Whatever form it takes, it needs to be understood by all those involved and properly evaluated (Barr and Hashagen, 2000).

Presented in this way, community development may be perceived as being wholly functional, a toolkit of knowledge, skills and techniques to be used in a variety of different ways. In one sense, this is accurate: community development seeks to facilitate change and development, and it should always be easily accessible.

However, there is a danger that this way of looking at community development may miss the point about its potential contribution. The bringing together of the concepts of caring communities and social inclusion holds the possibility of increasing the participation of citizens in groups and initiatives, which in turn can lead to the building of stronger communities. This outcome would have the effect of bringing the knowledge and methods of community development to bear on some of society's most vulnerable groups of people with the aim of encouraging those who are most dependent to have influence. It is this fundamental point that is illustrated in the four case studies in this report and which needs to inform future practice.

5 Recommendations

The policy and practice conclusions of the action-research summarised in the preceding section have action implications for all stakeholders involved in taking forward community care within a framework of social inclusion and building stronger communities:

- Government Ministers and civil servants

- local authority elected members, managers and practitioners

- user and community groups

- national training organisations and others responsible for developing and delivering training programmes.

The policies and strategies of all organisations in these categories need in future to be informed by the findings of the action-research. This relates to the 'massive changes' required of local authorities, referred to in Chapter 3, and the role of community development in contributing to change in a practical way. The action-research findings provide a basis for local authorities to take forward the issue of caring communities and social inclusion. Given the requirements placed on them by Best Value and community planning, the findings can be addressed within an active policy and organisational context. Underpinning this overall message are three specific recommendations.

Guidelines for good practice

To facilitate the development of caring communities within a social inclusion framework, good practice guidelines should be prepared for local authorities which explain (a) why local authorities and other public sector agencies should find ways of supporting local development and caring communities, and (b) why prescriptive approaches to working with communities should be avoided.

The guidelines should also include specific and practical points. They should draw upon examples from the action-research, such as the need to present plans using clear, jargon-free language and to hold meetings in informal settings. They could also make use of established good practice in community development and other fields, e.g. that a local area looking to take forward a community development approach should have a clearly identified officer to lead on its implementation.

The guidelines should be prepared by experts in community development and community care in collaboration with user organisations, engaging with the local government associations.

Training opportunities

Members of all groups participating in community-based initiatives aimed at supporting caring communities – senior managers, frontline workers, community leaders, users – need to be properly equipped in terms of their knowledge and skills. Accordingly, accessible and imaginative training opportunities should be made available as an integral part of planning and resourcing community initiatives. The following types of training are proposed for each of the target groups:

Senior managers

Seminars or one-day courses on key topics:

- principles and methods of participative planning

- ways of consulting and negotiating with stakeholders and participants

- how to foster a partnership approach committed to inter-agency and interprofessional practice

- managing conflict, diversity and change

- developing and implementing participative approaches to accessing and managing resources

- devising policies, structures and programmes that promote social inclusion

- providing and promoting empowering leadership

- how to foster a participative culture committed to organisational learning

- how to use participative evaluation to inform strategic and operational practice. (Community Learning Scotland, 1998)

Frontline workers

Short courses supported by consultancy assistance on:

- understanding core components of community development in the context of social inclusion and caring communities

- skills development on how to work on a locality basis, with communities of interest and within organisations.

Community leaders and users

Short courses supported by consultancy on:

- knowing how to assess community needs

- group work

- effective partnerships.

Dialogue and joined-up policy

The importance of recognising community care users as a potentially excluded population requires a dialogue at both national and local levels between policymakers responsible for community care and those who are developing social inclusion programmes – with practitioners, community leader, users and carers. It is recommended that:

- A national policy seminar is held at which the findings and recommendations of the action-research are discussed. Its purpose would be to clarify ways of taking forward the challenge of caring communities within a social inclusion framework.

- Local authorities which are planning a community development approach to community care are urged to start by holding policy conferences to which all stakeholders would be invited. Their purpose would be to clarify the overall framework within which any initiative or programme is to be developed.

Note

Chapter 2

1 The other option related to development of community
   participation in care planning in a peripheral housing scheme.
   This work was undertaken anyway and led to the creation of the
   Castlemilk Locality Panel, itself a good example of community
   development approaches to community care that has won a
   good practice award from the Convention of Scottish Local
   Authorities.

References

Barr, A., Drysdale, J. and Henderson, P. (1997) *Towards Caring Communities*. Brighton: Pavilion Publishing

Barr, A., Drysdale, J. and Henderson, P. (1998) 'Realising the potential of community care – the role of community development', *Issues in Social Work Education*, Vol. 18, No. 1

Barr, A. and Hashagen, S. (2000) *Achieving Better Community Development. A Handbook for Planning and Evaluation*. London: CDF Publications

Community Learning Scotland (1998) *Guidelines for Post Qualifying Community Practice and Development Training, CeVe Guidelines Series*, No. 8. Edinburgh: Community Learning Scotland

Filkin, G. with Lord Bassam, Corrigan, P., Stoker, G. and Tizard, J. (1999) *Starting to Modernise*. London: New Local Government Network

Foong, A.L.S. and Walsh, B. (1995) *Mental Health Services and the Experience of the Elderly Chinese Community*. London: Royal College of Nursing/Thames Valley University

Henderson, P. and Mayo, M. (1998) *Training and Education in Urban Regeneration*. Bristol: The Policy Press

Henderson, P. and Salmon, H. (2000) *Social Exclusion and Community Development: Promises and Potential*. London: CDF Publications

Joseph Rowntree Foundation (1999) 'Evaluation of the National User Involvement Project', *Findings* (January), No. 129. York: Joseph Rowntree Foundation

Lister, R. (1999) 'First steps to a fairer society'. *The Guardian*, 9 June

Taylor, M. (1995) 'Community work and the state: the changing context of UK practice', in G. Craig and M. Mayo (eds) *Community Empowerment*. London: Zed Books, pp. 99–111

Appendix 1: Background to the action-research

This report of an action-research project builds on the findings of a research and training project funded primarily by the Joseph Rowntree Foundation and completed in 1997. That project developed a training pack and resource book based on the evidence of case studies of the application and benefits of community development principles and methods in the field of community care (Barr *et al.*, 1997, 1998).These were summarised as:

- empowered users organisations
- better services
- greater consumer satisfaction.
- supportive communities
- community regeneration.

These were seen as products of:

- a user defined, needs-led approach
- more effective use of community resources identified on agreed needs
- mobilising of community leadership and action
- improving networking between users, communities and agencies
- developing transferable knowledge and skills of participants
- achieving changes in power leading to (a) greater accountability of service providers to users and (b) community led provision and engagement with policy planning

- achieving changes in attitudes to, and practices of, user participation

- establishing new forms of provision

- adequately resourcing local communities to contribute effectively to care provision

While the case studies had provided convincing evidence of the potential of a community development approach, there was little indication that mainstream service agencies were adopting the approach, despite, in some cases, having a clear policy. Nonetheless, the dissemination events had indicated a high level of interest within local authorities and voluntary organisations. It was agreed, therefore, to test the potential of the approach in mainstream agencies.

Funding was provided by the Joseph Rowntree Foundation and the Scottish Office Social Work Services Inspectorate for a three-year action-research study located in four sites in Scotland. It was agreed that the project needed to be relevant to the UK as a whole. This was reflected in the composition of the advisory group. The project, which ran from April 1997 to March 2000, had a combined budget of £75,000 over three years to cover action support to the projects, collection of research data, analysis and write-up, plus meetings with and reporting to the sponsors and advisory group. The staffing consisted of: part of the time of three staff based at the Scottish Community Development Centre in Glasgow (Alan Barr throughout the project and in years 1 and 2 Jacky Drysdale and year 3 Carolyn Stenhouse) and of one from the Community Development Foundation based in Leeds (Paul Henderson). Direct project support work was conducted through the Scottish-based staff.

Project sites were selected following consultation with local agencies and community organisations. The criteria used for selection were:

- that there was a commitment by statutory or voluntary organisations to applying the necessary resources – human and material – to support the development

- that community development approaches to community care were not yet well established in the agency

- that there was existing support to user organisations and networks

- that there was a willingness to establish partnerships with users in the development of services

- that there was a policy commitment to extensive user involvement and equal opportunities

- that there was a commitment, not only to the training and consultancy support, but, equally, to the monitoring and evaluation aspects of the programme

- that there was a commitment to adjusting policy and practice in the light of lessons from the project

- that there was a willingness to participate in dissemination events irrespective of whether the initiative was evaluated as successful.

The projects were selected on the basis that these preconditions would be likely to foster successful development. In each of the partnership agencies, there was a recognition that community care is more than simply a set of services provided for vulnerable people in the community but relates also to the rights and obligations of citizenship and encapsulates a much more active relationship between people and their communities.

The action-research method meant that, throughout the project, research team members were active participant observers of events and actions that they helped to initiate or develop. They had a strong commitment to successful outcomes based on principles and values of community development and social inclusion. They brought with them a critical perspective based on these commitments but sought to base their analysis on systematic collection of data reflecting the perspectives of all the key participants.

Appendix 2: Research methods and data sources

- *Baseline questionnaires.* These explored the perceptions of those involved in each local project at its start. The main themes were: the purpose of the project, the factors which would enable it to achieve its goals and the problems which would need to be addressed to improve the likelihood of success.

- *Participant observation.* Throughout the project the researchers had regular involvement with the steering groups for each of the projects and facilitated, contributed to or attended a range of events. The work was recorded throughout these processes including detailed interim progress reports for each project.

- *Project records.* Each project kept its own records of meetings and decisions, and there were several internal progress reports. These were available to the researchers.

- *Focus groups/Workshops.* At the end of the second year, all of the projects were brought together for a cross-site workshop that explored the factors which participants felt had been most influential in the development of the projects. At the end of the project, a one-day review workshop was conducted with the main participants on each site. This explored what participants felt had been achieved and why, what else could be achieved and how this might be done. (In some cases, interviews were also conducted with key participants who were unable to attend the final workshops.)

- *Key informant interviews.* On each site, a minimum of six interviews were conducted with individuals identified as beneficiaries of the project. In some cases, these were service users and in others officials. Their common characteristic was that they had not been directly involved in the project but were seen by the participants as key people whom the project set out to benefit or influence.

- *Final questionnaire.* A questionnaire tailored to reflect the characteristics of each project was sent to all the active participants in the steering groups for the projects. This echoed the content of the baseline questionnaire and focused on the successes and failures of the project, the reasons for these and the lessons that participants had taken from the project. The questionnaires were used as a trigger for discussion in the final review workshops.

- *Case study.* In Glasgow, as the researchers could not participate directly in the local meetings of the Asian carers group, they prepared a case study based on interviews and focus groups with both the carers and agency staff.

Appendix 3: Members of Advisory Group

Waquar Ahmed, Professor of Primary Care Research, University of Leeds

Andrena Cumella, Fellow, Office for Public Management

Etienne d'Aboville, Manager, Centre for Independent Living, Glasgow

Marjorie Mayo, Reader, Goldsmiths College, University of London

Rab Murray, Depute Director of Social Work, Glasgow City Council

Alex O'Neil (Chair), Principal Research Manager, Social Care and Disability, Joseph Rowntree Foundation

Ian Robertson, Assistant Chief Inspector, Scottish Executive Social Work Services Inspectorate

Neil Small, Professor of Community and Primary Care, University of Bradford

Professor David Ward, Professor of Social Work, Department of Social and Community Studies, De Montfort University

David Wiseman, Head of Strategic Services, South Lanarkshire Council